D0095192

# The
# Love Poems
# of Lord Byron

George Gordon, Lord Byron

# The
# Love Poems
# of Lord Byron

*A Romantic's Passion*

*Selected and with an
Introduction by
David Stanford Burr*

St. Martin's Press
New York

*Production Editor: David Stanford Burr*

*Design by Glen M. Edelstein*

**Library of Congress Cataloging-in-Publication Data**

Byron, George Gordon Byron, Baron, 1788–1824.
  The Love poems of Lord Byron : a romantic's passion / George Gordon, Lord Byron.
    p. cm.
   ISBN 0-312-05124-7
  1. Love poetry, English. I. Title.
 PR4353 1990
 821'.7—dc20           90-36879
                   CIP

10 9

# Contents

v

# Introduction

The voracious interest in Lord Byron's extraordinary career—the literary works, political endeavors, magnetic personality, and sensational private life—fueled by his death in 1824 has continued at a high level up to the present day. The scope of this collection of Byron's poetry is his short love lyrics, most of which are juvenilia. These youthful poems of literary merit and personal charm trace the evolution of Byron's poetry to the mature style of his later, longer works—the works that bear his claim as a great poet of the English language.

In selecting these forty-four poems I refrained from presenting thematic extracts from the longer, more famous works, believing that they would comprise too fragmentary an offering. The poems are presented in approximate chronological order of composition with further commentary following the text in a Notes section. Accompanying the poems are selected portraits of the significant women in Byron's life. The following brief biography is provided so that the reader might appreciate the circumstances leading to the composition of these largely autobiographical poems.

In 1785 George Gordon Byron's prodigal father, Captain John "Mad Jack" Byron, took for his second wife Catherine Gordon, a Scottish heiress; he managed to squander her fortune by George's birth in London on January 22, 1788, and died in 1791 in France. The nearly destitute Catherine was devoted to George and sought expert medical advice for her son's congenital clubbed right foot and provided for his proper education at the Aberdeen Grammar School, where he read the Old Testament "through & through."

In 1798, at the age of ten, George became the sixth Baron Byron of Rochdale with the death of his granduncle William. The ancestral estate, Newstead Abbey, in Nottinghamshire, which contained part of Sherwood Forest, proved a great delight to the young lord with its fields, forests, lakes, Gothic abbey, and palatial manor.

In 1799 George received painful treatments for his clubfoot by a quack practitioner and also suffered mistreatments by the alcoholic governess that included neglect, physical abuse, and sexual advances. Finally, an anatomist prescribed a corrective boot, and the governess was dismissed. In 1801 Byron was sent to Harrow, the renowned public school for the scions of the aristocracy as well as the middle class, and reproved those who taunted his lameness with his fists and a gameness for sports, especially swimming, at which he excelled. His sentiments lay with the underdog, and he became a champion of the younger boys, several of whom he initiated into passionate relationships. The sexual extent of these Harrovian attachments is unclear to Byron's biographers. After his Eastern Tour there would be no question of his bisexuality; however, his emotional satisfaction would be largely derived from women. It is also unclear how early Byron began to pen verse—certainly by age twelve. While at Harrow he scribbled epigrams, satires, and secretly pursued more serious poetic efforts.

The fifteen-year-old lord fell in love with his neighbor and distant cousin, the eighteen-year-old beauty Mary Chaworth, the subject of the amorous poem "To Emma" who would soon become engaged and married. Byron then began an intimate correspondence with Augusta Byron, his half sister, four years his senior. Augusta and Byron had been raised separately and Byron drew closer to her as his excitable mother became more and more temperamental. In 1805 he entered Trinity College of Cambridge University, but he preferred London and skipped a term while directing his attention to the completion, private printing, and private circulation of a small volume of poems, *Fugitive Pieces*. This collection of juvenilia contained romantic, melancholic, realistic, satiric, and erotic lyrics. "To a Lady Who Presented to the Author a Lock of Hair Braided with His Own, and Appointed a Night in December to Meet Him in the Garden" indicates the later tenor of Byron's sophisticated seriocomic works.

At Cambridge, Byron had little trouble from his clubfoot, but the effects of debauchery had become apparent, and by the fall of 1806 his five-foot-eight-and-one-half-inch frame was carrying over two hundred pounds. Adopting a vigorous regimen of exercise, dieting, and "taking physic," he regained and maintained his handsome slenderness for the next twelve years. In June of 1807 *Hours of Idleness* was publicly printed. This undistinguished offering was largely derived from eighteenth-century Romantic and neoclassical sources and indicates Byron's clear veneration for the Augustan age and Alexander Pope. Byron's Cantabrigian circle of young intellectuals and political liberals provided some long-lasting friendships that withstood his decided unconventionality: he scoffed at the school rule forbidding the keeping of dogs by keeping a tame bear in the turret above his quarters.

In 1807, with Cambridge behind him, Byron settled in London, quite comfortable in the role of nobleman bard, dandy, and hedonist. Due to the military situation on the Continent, he opted for an Eastern Tour over the usual Grand Tour of Europe after his upcoming twenty-first birthday. February 1808 brought a savage—though not entirely unjust—review of *Hours of Idleness* in the *Edinburgh Review*, and Byron, shocked out of the occasional and sentimental poesy of his first two collections, sought revenge by undertaking the Augustan mode of moral censure, pouring out his spleen into *English Bards and Scottish Reviewers*, the work that first clearly indicated Byron's métier. This Popean satire of over one thousand lines in heroic couplets comprises his first major work— a work of vitality and wit that though published anonymously was recognized immediately as Byron's. Praised by poets and printed through four editions, Byron would later view his "Dunciad" as a youthful satire that went too far, that attacked men he would later respect, and he suppressed a fifth edition of the diatribe. Meanwhile, Byron had taken his master's degree at Cambridge as well as his seat in the House of Lords, where with his liberal Whig sympathies he hoped, in time, to pursue a Parliamentary career.

On July 2, 1809, Byron set sail for Lisbon with his good friend and future groomsman, John Cam Hobhouse. His Eastern Tour crossed Spain (during the Peninsular War), visited Seville, Cadiz, Gibraltar, on to Geneva, and then to Albania where he enjoyed the hospitality of Ali Pasha's sumptuous Oriental court, which would provide characters and costumes for use in his Eastern Tales. After reading a selection of Edmund Spenser's *The Faerie Queene*, Byron concluded that the Spenserian stanza (a nine-line stanza with an *ababbcbcc* rhyming scheme where the first eight lines are iambic pentameter and the ninth is iambic hexameter) would provide the appropriate metric for his semiautobiographical poetic travelogue, and, accordingly, he began *Childe Harold's Pilgrimage*, finishing the First Canto in Athens by the end of the year.

In Athens he stayed at the home of a widow and her three lovely daughters; the youngest, twelve-year-old Theresa Macri, he would celebrate as "The Maid of Athens." The Acropolis, that citadel of ancient glory and democracy, proved a dispiriting contrast to Byron given the passive toleration of Turkish hegemony by the modern Greeks. Also indignant at the British plunder of classical treasures, Byron wrote the satiric *The Curse of Minerva*, vilifying Lord Elgin for removing the Parthenon Marbles to England. His visit to the plain of Marathon, the site of a great Athenian victory over the invading Persians in 490 B.C., would later be commemorated with philhellenic zeal in that stanza from *Don Juan* that contains the elegiac line: "I dreamed that Greece might still be free."

Leaving Theresa and the handsome sixteen-year-old Nicolo Giraud in Athens, Byron continued his Eastern Tour and arrived at Smyrna, where he finished the Second Canto. In imitation of Leander, the legendary lover of Hero, Byron swam the swift current of the Hellespont. He visited Constantinople with its bazaars, seraglios of odalisques, and sumptuous palaces that would color his later Oriental Tales. In July 1811, after two years of travel, Byron returned to England—with a stopover in Malta for treatment of gonorrhea—as a cosmopolitan with a particular appreciation for the insularity of his motherland.

In London Byron found a publisher for *Childe Harold*. Then came the shocking news of his mother's illness and swift death as well as the deaths of two of his best schoolboy friends and that of John Edleston, a former chorister at Trinity, whom Byron maintained he "loved more than I ever loved a living thing." In 1812 Byron gave his maiden speech in the House of Lords, an impassioned plea for leniency that opposed a Tory riot bill providing for the death penalty for unemployed Nottingham weavers who destroyed the looms that had superseded them. A few days after the publication of *Childe Harold* on March 10, Byron said, "I awoke one morning and found myself famous." The poem was widely lionized, its author became the most sought-after personality by fashionable London society, and the reading public quickly chose to identify Harold, the melancholic and cynical protagonist, with the author.

The eccentric, and married, Lady Caroline Lamb doggedly pursued Byron, and their developing affair soon proved disgusting to Byron, who offered marriage to the humorless Annabella Milbanke as an escape from Lady Caroline. Miss Milbanke refused, and Byron began planning another Mediterranean adventure. In June 1813 he began an affair with his half sister and longtime correspondent, Augusta Leigh, who was the unhappily married mother of three daughters. Byron was both fascinated and repelled by their liaison.

The popular demand for Byron's romantic poetry led him to begin a series of Eastern Tales that furthered the myth of the Byronic Hero, the outlaw-hero, in England and on the Continent. *The Giaour*, *The Bride of Abydos* (with its brother-sister incest theme), and *The Corsair* were written quickly and devoured avidly by the public. The colorful Levantine scenery continues in *Lara*, *Parsina*, and *The Siege of Corinth*, written in 1814 and 1815. On April 15, 1814, Augusta gave birth to a daughter, Elizabeth Medora, and Byron, declining acknowledgment of her paternity, pressed his suit of marriage on Annabella, whom he felt would provide a stabilizing domesticity.

After some curious dilatoriness by Byron, the two were married on January 2, 1815. Byron introduced Augusta to Annabella who soon realized the nature of his consanguine affection. In April, *Hebrew Melodies*, Byron's lyrics for Isaac Nathan's music, was published. Byron was greatly aggravated by ongoing estate litigation and disaffected with Parliament and the Tory government's desire to restore European pre-Napoleonic status quo. The pregnant Lady Byron and Augusta believed Byron's dark rages were indicative of temporary insanity. On December 10, 1815, Augusta Ada was born, and on January 15, 1816, Lady Byron took Ada and returned to her parents' home; the amiable separation turned sour when her parents became acquainted with Byron's mistreatment of his wife and the suspicion of incest. The scandal became public. Byron was snubbed socially, his library was auctioned to satisfy creditors, and the separation was finalized on April 21. The tender poem "Fare Thee Well" indicates his sense of loss at their failed marriage.

Before he left for the Continent for self-imposed exile, Byron developed a casual liaison with the persistent eighteen-year-old Claire Clairmont. Tired of his verse narratives and the public presumption that the Byronic Hero was a mirror image of himself, Byron added further installments to *Childe Harold*. In Geneva Byron met and became fast friends with Percy Shelley and was joined by the now pregnant Claire. Byron penned the best of the verse tales, *The Prisoner of Chillon*, and Canto III of *Childe Harold*, in which the hero-protagonist articulates Byron's wrongs and sufferings, his ostracism by a hypocritical English society, and his detestation of despotism. When he wrote "Stanzas to Augusta" he did not realize that back in England Lady Byron, jealous of Byron's affection for Augusta, was vigorously pursuing a cruel campaign to ruin her.

The next Byronic offering was *Manfred*, a blank-verse morality play about guilt and remorse—the incest theme again—that ends in stoic, dignified death. By the end of 1816 Byron was ensconced in the literary and social circle of Venice, while in England publication of Canto III and *The Prisoner of Chillon and Other Poems* reclaimed his former audience. On January 12 Clara Allegra Byron was born to Claire. After a round of debauchery during the pre-

Lenten Carnival, Byron wrote the lovely lyric "So We'll Go No More A-Roving." He began to work on Canto IV, which represented a transition to a more authentic mode of reflection and idiom. Byron's quest for artistic maturity came to fruition in *Beppo*, a wry satire that blended colloquial English, the flexible *ottava rima* (an eight-line stanza in iambic pentameter with an *abababcc* rhyme scheme), and comic, ironic digressions. Byron's Venetian palazzo was transformed into a personal harem of middle- and lower-class women as well as a menagerie for pet animals, and Margarita Cogni, a baker's wife, became his passionate inamorata and housekeeper for two years. His dissipation—including another brush with gonorrhea—led to weight gain, and Byron continued his prodigious literary output. By July, 1818, he had begun *Don Juan* (Byron anglicized Juan to rhyme with "true one"), his revision of the old Spanish legend where the protagonist is a handsome rogue who *is* the prey of womankind.

In April, 1819, the beautiful Countess Teresa Guiccioli attracted Byron's amorous attention and he became her *cavalier servente*, the furtive lover of a married woman whose husband, according to the contemporary Italian conventions of courtly love, should not be jealous. *Mazeppa* and the first two cantos of *Don Juan* were published; the latter met with fierce denunciation and charges of blasphemy and obscenity, but Byron believed epic-satire was his appropriate poetic vehicle and expressed surprise that the moral temper was so rigid as to be blind to his humorous intention.

Byron, disgusted with the ruthless repression of political reform in England, came to support the Italian insurrectionist Carbonari movement against Austrian rule. In his political dramas, *Marino Faliero*, *The Two Foscari*, and *Sardanapalus*, Byron eschewed the Gothic and reverted to the Classical Unities with the foredoomed intention of vitalizing the English stage. The Pope granted Teresa a separation from her husband, and Byron was made an honorary chief of the Carbonari, which he supplied with arms and money. Accordingly, the Austrian secret police began to monitor his movements, and Byron placed the four-year-old Allegra in a convent near Ravenna to avoid the expected revolution. The revolt failed and Teresa temporarily prevailed upon Byron to discontinue *Don Juan*, which she felt would only further tarnish his reputation. His philhellenism was fired by the news of the March, 1821, outbreak of the Greek War of Independence. The next work was a metaphysical drama, *Cain*, followed by *The Vision of Judgment*, Byron's sharply focused masterpiece of hilarious ridicule of Poet Laureate Robert Southey's poetic commemoration of the burial and, supposed, ascent to heaven of the tyrannical George III.

In Pisa, Teresa and Byron, now thirty-four, enjoyed the company of Shelley, a great admirer of *Don Juan*. Byron's mother-in-law, Lady Noel, died on January 28, 1822, leaving Byron a substantial portion of her estate; he took up the Noel arms and henceforth signed himself Noel Byron. Then on April 20 Allegra died of typhus fever and Byron shipped her body to England for burial, and on July 18 Shelley's drowned body washed ashore after his boat, *Don Juan*, capsized in a storm. Byron completed *The Age of Bronze*, another satire, this time against war profiteering in England, and also completed the sixteenth canto of *Don Juan* and began a seventeenth. Fully resolved to assist the Greeks in their War of Independence, Byron offered his services to the London Greek Committee, which elected him as a representative. He was hesitant to leave Teresa and the prolific writing to which he had become accustomed, but he felt morally bound to provide what service he could to the fledgling cause of Hellenic liberty.

On August 3, 1823, Byron landed at Cephalonia in a brigantine that he had secured and laden with medical supplies purchased with his own funds. The Greek factionalism and lack of discipline exasperated Byron, but he maintained his patience and demonstrated skill at handling the complex logistic and strategic realities of a military and political campaign. He made a personal loan to the Greek government of £4,000 to encourage the Greek fleet to attempt to emerge and break the Turkish blockade of the strategic town of Missolonghi. Byron sailed through the blockade and landed at the swampy Missolonghi on December 20, 1823, where he was received with a twenty-one gun salute and a hero's welcome. On January 22 he wrote one of his last poems, "On This Day I Complete My Thirty-Sixth Year," which echoes his earlier fatalistic presentiment. The Greeks wanted him to provide financing and to lead the attack on the Turkish stronghold of Lepanto, but insufficient forces caused him to delay the attack.

On February 15 Byron suffered a seizure, probably apoplectic, and his condition worsened with an inept leeching procedure. In England, the new cantos of *Don Juan* were well received as were the reports of the author's bold adventures. The cold, rainy weather delayed his campaign against Lepanto and the Greek fleet sailed away. He died on April 19, 1824, from uremic poisoning and further leeching. News of Byron's death was met with shocked disbelief in England and on the Continent, where his self-sacrifice and love of liberty would make him the epitome of Romanticism. He was applauded as a national hero in Greece, and his "martyrdom" was to lead directly to Greek liberty. The embalmed body was shipped to England, where it was laid to rest in the family vault in Hucknall Torkard Church near Newstead Abbey.

Byron's forte was the epic satire and *Don Juan* is his chef d'oeuvre. He had intended the poem to run to twenty-four cantos but only completed sixteen; there was no preliminary plan of poetic composition, rather the poem dictated its own direction. This large fragment has as its sources the Italian "burlesque" poetry, the picaresque novel, the eighteenth-century English novel, and the Classic epic. The versatile *ottava rima* allowed Byron a rich range of diction, and his wide travel, keen observation, and breadth of reading provided ample material for his Chaucerian narrative. The main theme of this spiritual autobiography was the conflict between Nature and Civilization with the accompanying secondary themes of the futility and inhumanity of war, military vainglory, the materialism and grundyism of English society, the hypocrisy of conventional marriage, and the ephemerality of natural love. His use of comic incongruity, commonsense moralism, and sharp realism makes him the most modern of the Romantic poets.

—DAVID STANFORD BURR
New York City
March 1990

# The
# Love Poems
# of Lord Byron

Newstead Abbey

## *To Caroline*

Think'st thou I saw thy beauteous eyes,
　　Suffused in tears, implore to stay;
And heard unmoved thy plenteous sighs,
　　Which said far more than words can say?

Though keen the grief thy tears exprest,
　　When love and hope lay both o'erthrown;
Yet still, my girl, this bleeding breast
　　Throbb'd with deep sorrow as thine own.

But when our cheeks with anguish glow'd,
　　When thy sweet lips were join'd to mine,
The tears that from my eyelids flow'd
　　Were lost in those which fell from thine.

Thou couldst not feel my burning cheek,
　　Thy gushing tears had quench'd its flame;
And as thy tongue essay'd to speak,
　　In sighs alone it breathed my name.

And yet, my girl, we weep in vain,
　　In vain our fate in sighs deplore;
Remembrance only can remain,—
　　But that will make us weep the more.

Again, thou best beloved, adieu!
    Ah! if thou canst, o'ercome regret;
Nor let thy mind past joys review,—
    Our only hope is to forget!

## *To Caroline*

When I hear you express an affection so warm,
    Ne'er think, my beloved, that I do not believe;
For your lip would the soul of suspicion disarm,
    And your eye beams a ray which can never deceive.

Yet, still, this fond bosom regrets, while adoring,
    That love, like the leaf, must fall into the sear;
That age will come on, when remembrance, deploring,
    Contemplates the scenes of her youth with a tear;

That the time must arrive, when, no longer retaining
    Their auburn, those locks must wave thin to the breeze,
When a few silver hairs of those tresses remaining
    Prove nature a prey to decay and disease.

'T is this, my beloved, which spreads gloom o'er my features,
    Though I ne'er shall presume to arraign the decree,
Which God has proclaim'd as the fate of his creatures,
    In the death which one day will deprive you of me.

Mistake not, sweet sceptic, the cause of emotion,
    No doubt can the mind of your lover invade;
He worships each look with such faithful devotion,
    A smile can enchant, or a tear can dissuade.

2

But as death, my beloved, soon or late shall o'ertake us,
    And our breasts, which alive with such sympathy glow,
Will sleep in the grave till the blast shall awake us,
    When calling the dead, in earth's bosom laid low,—

Oh! then let us drain, while we may, draughts of pleasure,
    Which from passion like ours may unceasingly flow;
Let us pass round the cup of love's bliss in full measure,
    And quaff the contents as our nectar below.


### Imitated from Catullus

## To Ellen

Oh! might I kiss those eyes of fire,
A million scarce would quench desire:
Still would I steep my lips in bliss,
And dwell an age on every kiss;
Nor then my soul should sated be,
Still would I kiss and cling to thee:
Nought should my kiss from thine dissever;
Still would we kiss, and kiss for ever,
E'en though the numbers did exceed
The yellow harvest's countless seed.
To part would be a vain endeavour:
Could I desist?—ah! never—never!

## From Anacreon

Θέλω λέγειν Ἀτρείδας, κ. τ. λ.

I wish to tune my quivering lyre
To deeds of fame and notes of fire;
To echo, from its rising swell,
How heroes fought and nations fell,
When Atreus' sons advanced to war,
Or Tyrian Cadmus roved afar;
But still, to martial strains unknown,
My lyre recurs to love alone.
Fired with the hope of future fame,
I seek some nobler hero's name;
The dying chords are strung anew,
To war, to war, my harp is due.
With glowing strings, the epic strain
To Jove's great son I raise again;
Alcides and his glorious deeds,
Beneath whose arm the Hydra bleeds.
All, all in vain; my wayward lyre
Wakes silver notes of soft desire.
Adieu, ye chiefs renown'd in arms!
Adieu the clang of war's alarms!
To other deeds my soul is strung,
And sweeter notes shall now be sung;
My harp shall all its powers reveal,
To tell the tale my heart must feel;
Love, Love alone, my lyre shall claim,
In songs of bliss and sighs of flame.

## To Emma

Since now the hour is come at last,
  When you must quit your anxious lover;
Since now our dream of bliss is past,
  One pang, my girl, and all is over.

Alas! that pang will be severe,
  Which bids us part to meet no more;
Which tears me far from one so dear,
  Departing for a distant shore.

Well! we have pass'd some happy hours,
  And joy will mingle with our tears;
When thinking on these ancient towers,
  The shelter of our infant years;

Where from this Gothic casement's height,
  We view'd the lake, the park, the dell,
And still, though tears obstruct our sight,
  We lingering look a last farewell,

O'er fields through which we used to run,
  And spend the hours in childish play;
O'er shades where, when our race was done,
  Reposing on my breast you lay;

Whilst I, admiring, too remiss,
  Forgot to scare the hovering flies,
Yet envied every fly the kiss
  It dared to give your slumbering eyes:

See still the little painted bark,
  In which I row'd you o'er the lake;
See there, high waving o'er the park,
  The elm I clamber'd for your sake.

These times are past—our joys are gone,
　　You leave me, leave this happy vale;
These scenes I must retrace alone:
　　Without thee what will they avail?

Who can conceive, who has not proved,
　　The anguish of a last embrace?
When, torn from all you fondly loved,
　　You bid a long adieu to peace.

This is the deepest of our woes,
　　For this these tears our cheeks bedew;
This is of love the final close,
　　Oh, God! the fondest, last adieu!

## To M. S. G.

Whene'er I view those lips of thine,
　　Their hue invites my fervent kiss;
Yet I forego that bliss divine,
　　Alas, it were unhallow'd bliss!

Whene'er I dream of that pure breast,
　　How could I dwell upon its snows!
Yet is the daring wish repress'd,
　　For that—would banish its repose.

A glance from thy soul-searching eye
　　Can raise with hope, depress with fear;
Yet I conceal my love—and why?
　　I would not force a painful tear.

I ne'er have told my love, yet thou
    Hast seen my ardent flame too well;
And shall I plead my passion now,
    To make thy bosom's heaven a hell?

No! for thou never canst be mine,
    United by the priest's decree:
By any ties but those divine,
    Mine, my beloved, thou ne'er shalt be.

Then let the secret fire consume,
    Let it consume, thou shalt not know:
With joy I court a certain doom,
    Rather than spread its guilty glow.

I will not ease my tortured heart,
    By driving dove-eyed peace from thine;
Rather than such a sting impart,
    Each thought presumptuous I resign.

Yes! yield those lips, for which I'd brave
    More than I here shall dare to tell;
Thy innocence and mine to save,—
    I bid thee now a last farewell.

Yes! yield that breast, to see despair,
    And hope no more thy soft embrace;
Which to obtain my soul would dare,
    All, all reproach—but thy disgrace.

At least from guilt shalt thou be free,
    No matron shall thy shame reprove;
Though cureless pangs may prey on me,
    No martyr shalt thou be to love.

## The First Kiss of Love

'Α Βάρβιτος δὲ χορδαῖς
῎Ερωτα μοῦνον ἠχεῖ.
—Anacreon

Away with your fictions of flimsy romance,
　　Those tissues of falsehood which folly has wove!
Give me the mild beam of the soul-breathing glance,
　　Or the rapture which dwells on the first kiss of love.

Ye rhymers, whose bosoms with phantasy glow,
　　Whose pastoral passions are made for the grove;
From what blest inspiration your sonnets would flow,
　　Could you ever have tasted the first kiss of love!

If Apollo should e'er his assistance refuse,
　　Or the Nine be disposed from your service to rove,
Invoke them no more, bid adieu to the muse,
　　And try the effect of the first kiss of love.

I hate you, ye cold compositions of art!
　　Though prudes may condemn me, and bigots reprove,
I court the effusions that spring from the heart,
　　Which throbs with delight to the first kiss of love.

Your shepherds, your flocks, those fantastical themes,
　　Perhaps may amuse, yet they never can move:
Arcadia displays but a region of dreams;
　　What are visions like these to the first kiss of love?

Oh! cease to affirm that man, since his birth,
　　From Adam till now, has with wretchedness strove;
Some portion of paradise still is on earth,
　　And Eden revives in the first kiss of love.

When age chills the blood, when our pleasures are past—
    For years fleet away with the wings of the dove—
The dearest remembrance will still be the last,
    Our sweetest memorial the first kiss of love.

## To Woman

Woman! experience might have told me,
That all must love thee who behold thee:
Surely experience might have taught
Thy firmest promises are nought:
But, placed in all thy charms before me,
All I forget, but to adore thee.
Oh memory! thou choicest blessing
When join'd with hope, when still possessing;
But how much cursed by every lover
When hope is fled and passion's over.
Woman, that fair and fond deceiver,
How prompt are striplings to believe her!
How throbs the pulse when first we view
The eye that rolls in glossy blue,
Or sparkles black, or mildly throws
A beam from under hazel brows!
How quick we credit every oath,
And hear her plight the willing troth!
Fondly we hope 't will last for aye,
When, lo! she changes in a day.
This record will for ever stand,
"Woman, thy vows are traced in sand."

## To M. S. G.

When I dream that you love me, you'll surely forgive;
  Extend not your anger to sleep;
For in visions alone your affection can live,—
  I rise, and it leaves me to weep.

Then, Morpheus! envelope my faculties fast,
  Shed o'er me your languor benign;
Should the dream of to-night but resemble the last,
  What rapture celestial is mine!

They tell us that slumber, the sister of death,
  Mortality's emblem is given;
To fate how I long to resign my frail breath,
  If this be a foretaste of heaven!

Ah! frown not, sweet lady, unbend your soft brow,
  Nor deem me too happy in this;
If I sin in my dream, I atone for it now,
  Thus doom'd but to gaze upon bliss.

Though in visions, sweet lady, perhaps you may smile,
  Oh, think not my penance deficient!
When dreams of your presence my slumbers beguile,
  To awake will be torture sufficient.

Miss Mary Chaworth

## To Mary on Receiving Her Picture

This faint resemblance of thy charms,
   Though strong as mortal art could give,
My constant heart of fear disarms,
   Revives my hopes, and bids me live.

Here I can trace the locks of gold
   Which round thy snowy forehead wave,
The cheeks which sprung from beauty's mould,
   The lips which made me beauty's slave.

Here I can trace—ah, no! that eye,
   Whose azure floats in liquid fire,
Must all the painter's art defy,
   And bid him from the task retire.

Here I behold its beauteous hue;
   But where's the beam so sweetly straying,
Which gave a lustre to its blue,
   Like Luna o'er the ocean playing?

Sweet copy! far more dear to me,
   Lifeless, unfeeling as thou art,
Than all the living forms could be,
   Save her who placed thee next my heart.

She placed it, sad, with needless fear,
    Lest time might shake my wavering soul,
Unconscious that her image there
    Held every sense in fast control.

Through hours, through years, through time, 't will cheer;
    My hope in gloomy moments raise;
In life's last conflict 't will appear,
    And meet my fond expiring gaze.

### *To Lesbia*

Lesbia! since far from you I've ranged,
    Our souls with fond affection glow not;
You say 't is I, not you, have changed,
    I'd tell you why,—but yet I know not.

Your polish'd brow no cares have crost;
    And, Lesbia! we are not much older,
Since, trembling, first my heart I lost,
    Or told my love, with hope grown bolder.

Sixteen was then our utmost age,
    Two years have lingering past away, love!
And now new thoughts our minds engage,
    At least I feel disposed to stray, love!

'T is I that am alone to blame,
    I, that am guilty of love's treason;
Since your sweet breast is still the same,
    Caprice must be my only reason.

I do not, love! suspect your truth,
　　With jealous doubt my bosom heaves not;
Warm was the passion of my youth,
　　One trace of dark deceit it leaves not.

No, no, my flame was not pretended,
　　For, oh! I loved you most sincerely;
And—though our dream at last is ended—
　　My bosom still esteems you dearly.

No more we meet in yonder bowers;
　　Absence has made me prone to roving;
But older, firmer hearts than ours
　　Have found monotony in loving.

Your cheek's soft bloom is unimpair'd,
　　New beauties still are daily bright'ning,
Your eye for conquest beams prepared,
　　The forge of love's resistless lightning.

Arm'd thus, to make their bosoms bleed,
　　Many will throng to sigh like me, love!
More constant they may prove, indeed;
　　Fonder, alas! they ne'er can be, love!

### To A Lady Who Presented to the Author a Lock of Hair Braided with His Own, and Appointed a Night in December to Meet Him in the Garden

These locks, which fondly thus entwine,
In firmer chains our hearts confine
Than all th' unmeaning protestations
Which swell with nonsense love orations.
Our love is fix'd, I think we've proved it,
Nor time, nor place, nor art have moved it;
Then wherefore should we sigh and whine,
With groundless jealousy repine,
With silly whims and fancies frantic,
Merely to make our love romantic?
Why should you weep like Lydia Languish,
And fret with self-created anguish?
Or doom the lover you have chosen,
On winter nights to sigh half frozen;
In leafless shades to sue for pardon,
Only because the scene's a garden?
For gardens seem, by one consent
(Since Shakspeare set the precedent,
Since Juliet first declared her passion),
To form the place of assignation.
Oh! would some modern muse inspire,
And seat her by a sea-coal fire;
Or had the bard at Christmas written,
And laid the scene of love in Britain,
He surely, in commiseration,
Had changed the place of declaration.
In Italy I've no objection,
Warm nights are proper for reflection;
But here our climate is so rigid,

That love itself is rather frigid:
Think on our chilly situation,
And curb this rage for imitation.
Then let us meet, as oft we've done,
Beneath the influence of the sun;
Or, if at midnight I must meet you,
Within your mansion let me greet you:
There we can love for hours together,
Much better, in such snowy weather,
Than placed in all th' Arcadian groves
That ever witness'd rural loves;
Then, if my passion fail to please,
Next night I'll be content to freeze;
No more I'll give a loose to laughter,
But curse my fate for ever after.

### *Translation from the* Medea *of Euripides*

Ἔρωτες ὑπὲρ μὲν ἄγαν, κ. τ. λ.

When fierce conflicting passions urge
 The breast where love is wont to glow,
What mind can stem the stormy surge
 Which rolls the tide of human woe?
The hope of praise, the dread of shame,
 Can rouse the tortured breast no more;
The wild desire, the guilty flame,
 Absorbs each wish it felt before.

But if affection gently thrills
   The soul by purer dreams possest,
The pleasing balm of mortal ills
   In love can soothe the aching breast:
If thus thou comest in disguise,
   Fair Venus! from thy native heaven,
What heart unfeeling would despise
   The sweetest boon the gods have given?

But never from thy golden bow
   May I beneath the shaft expire!
Whose creeping venom, sure and slow,
   Awakes an all-consuming fire:
Ye racking doubts! ye jealous fears!
   With others wage internal war;
Repentance, source of future tears,
   From me be ever distant far!

May no distracting thoughts destroy
   The holy calm of sacred love!
May all the hours be wing'd with joy,
   Which hover faithful hearts above!
Fair Venus, on thy myrtle shrine
   May I with some fair lover sigh,
Whose heart may mingle pure with mine—
   With me to live, with me to die!

My native soil! beloved before,
   Now dearer as my peaceful home,
Ne'er may I quit thy rocky shore,
   A hapless banish'd wretch to roam!
This very day, this very hour,
   May I resign this fleeting breath;
Nor quit my silent humble bower,
   A doom to me far worse than death.

Have I not heard the exile's sigh?
    And seen the exile's silent tear,
Through distant climes condemn'd to fly,
    A pensive, weary wanderer here?
Ah, hapless dame! no sire bewails,
    No friend thy wretched fate deplores,
No kindred voice with rapture hails
    Thy steps within a stranger's doors.

Perish the fiend whose iron heart,
    To fair affection's truth unknown,
Bids her he fondly loved depart,
    Unpitied, helpless, and alone;
Who ne'er unlocks with silver key
    The milder treasures of his soul,—
May such a friend be far from me,
    And ocean's storms between us roll!


## To a Beautiful Quaker

Sweet girl! though only once we met,
That meeting I shall ne'er forget;
And though we ne'er may meet again,
Remembrance will thy form retain.
I would not say, "I love," but still
My senses struggle with my will:
In vain, to drive thee from my breast,
My thoughts are more and more represt;
In vain I check the rising sighs,
Another to the last replies:
Perhaps this is not love, but yet
Our meeting I can ne'er forget.

What though we never silence broke,
Our eyes a sweeter language spoke.

The tongue in flattering falsehood deals,
And tells a tale it never feels;
Deceit the guilty lips impart,
And hush the mandates of the heart;
But soul's interpreters, the eyes,
Spurn such restraint and scorn disguise.
As thus our glances oft conversed,
And all our bosoms felt, rehearsed,
No spirit, from within, reproved us,
Say rather, "'t was the spirit moved us."
Though what they utter'd I repress,
Yet I conceive thou'lt partly guess;
For as on thee my memory ponders,
Perchance to me thine also wanders.
This for myself, at least, I'll say,
Thy form appears through night, through day:
Awake, with it my fancy teems;
In sleep, it smiles in fleeting dreams;
The vision charms the hours away,
And bids me curse Aurora's ray
For breaking slumbers of delight
Which make me wish for endless night:
Since, oh! whate'er my future fate,
Shall joy or woe my steps await,
Tempted by love, by storms beset,
Thine image I can ne'er forget.


Alas! again no more we meet,
No more our former looks repeat;
Then let me breathe this parting prayer,
The dictate of my bosom's care:
"May Heaven so guard my lovely quaker,
That anguish never can o'ertake her;
That peace and virtue ne'er forsake her,
But bliss be aye her heart's partaker!

Oh, may the happy mortal, fated
To be by dearest ties related,
For her each hour new joys discover,
And lose the husband in the lover!
May that fair bosom never know
What 't is to feel the restless woe
Which stings the soul with vain regret,
Of him who never can forget!"


## To a Lady Who Presented the Author with the Velvet Band which Bound Her Tresses

This Band, which bound thy yellow hair,
    Is mine, sweet girl! thy pledge of love;
It claims my warmest, dearest care,
    Like relics left of saints above.

Oh! I will wear it next my heart;
    'T will bind my soul in bonds to thee;
From me again 't will ne'er depart,
    But mingle in the grave with me.

The dew I gather from thy lip
    Is not so dear to me as this;
*That* I but for a moment sip,
    And banquet on a transient bliss:

*This* will recall each youthful scene,
   E'en when our lives are on the wane;
The leaves of Love will still be green
   When Memory bids them bud again.

Oh! little lock of golden hue,
   In gently waving ringlet curl'd,
By the dear head on which you grow,
   I would not lose you for a world.

Not though a thousand more adorn
   The polish'd brow where once you shone,
Like rays which gild a cloudless morn,
   Beneath Columbia's fervid zone.


## To a Lady

Oh! had my fate been join'd with thine,
   As once this pledge appear'd a token,
These follies had not then been mine,
   For then my peace had not been broken.

To thee these early faults I owe,
   To thee, the wise and old reproving:
They know my sins, but do not know
   'T was thine to break the bonds of loving.

For once my soul, like thine, was pure,
   And all its rising fires could smother;
But now thy vows no more endure,
   Bestow'd by thee upon another.

Perhaps his peace I could destroy,
    And spoil the blisses that await him;
Yet let my rival smile in joy,
    For thy dear sake I cannot hate him.

Ah! since thy angel form is gone,
    My heart no more can rest with any;
But what it sought in thee alone,
    Attempts, alas! to find in many.

Then fare thee well, deceitful maid!
    'T were vain and fruitless to regret thee;
Nor Hope, nor Memory yield their aid,
    But Pride may teach me to forget thee.

Yet all this giddy waste of years,
    This tiresome round of palling pleasures;
These varied loves, these matron's fears,
    These thoughtless strains to passion's measures—

If thou wert mine, had all been hush'd:—
    This cheek now pale from early riot,
With passion's hectic ne'er had flush'd,
    But bloom'd in calm domestic quiet.

Yes, once the rural scene was sweet,
    For Nature seem'd to smile before thee;
And once my breast abhorr'd deceit,—
    For then it beat but to adore thee.

But now I seek for other joys:
    To think would drive my soul to madness;
In thoughtless throngs and empty noise,
    I conquer half my bosom's sadness.

Yet, even in these a thought will steal,
  In spite of every vain endeavour;
And fiends might pity what I feel,—
  To know that thou art lost for ever.


## To Anne

Oh, Anne! your offences to me have been grievous;
  I thought from my wrath no atonement could save you;
But woman is made to command and deceive us—
  I look'd in your face, and I almost forgave you.

I vow'd I could ne'er for a moment respect you,
  Yet thought that a day's separation was long;
When we met, I determined again to suspect you—
  Your smile soon convinced me suspicion was wrong.

I swore, in a transport of young indignation,
  With fervent contempt evermore to disdain you:
I saw you—my anger became admiration;
  And now, all my wish, all my hope's to regain you.

With beauty like yours, oh, how vain the contention,
  Thus lowly I sue for forgiveness before you;—
At once to conclude such a fruitless dissension,
  Be false, my sweet Anne, when I cease to adore you!

## On Finding a Fan

In one who felt as once he felt,
  This might, perhaps, have fann'd the flame;
But now his heart no more will melt,
  Because that heart is not the same.

As when the ebbing flames are low,
  The aid which once improved their light
And bade them burn with fiercer glow,
  Now quenches all their blaze in night,

Thus has it been with passion's fires—
  As many a boy and girl remembers—
While every hope of love expires,
  Extinguish'd with the dying embers.

The *first*, though not a spark survive,
  Some careful hand may teach to burn;
The *last*, alas! can ne'er survive,
  No touch can bid its warmth return.

Or, if it chance to wake again,
  Not always doom'd its heat to smother,
It sheds (so wayward fates ordain)
  Its former warmth around another.

## Song

Breeze of the night in gentler sighs
   More softly murmur o'er the pillow;
For Slumber seals my Fanny's eyes,
   And Peace must never shun her pillow.

Or breathe those sweet Æolian strains
   Stolen from celestial spheres above,
To charm her ear while some remains,
   And soothe her soul to dreams of love.

But Breeze of night again forbear,
   In softest murmurs only sigh;
Let not a Zephyr's pinion dare
   To lift those auburn locks on high.

Chill is thy Breath thou breeze of night!
   Oh! ruffle not those lids of Snow;
For only Morning's cheering light
   May wake the beam that lurks below.

Blest be that lip and azure eye!
   Sweet Fanny, hallow'd be thy Sleep!
Those lips shall never vent a sigh,
   Those eyes may never wake to weep.

## "When We Two Parted"

When we two parted
  In silence and tears,
Half broken-hearted
  To sever for years,
Pale grew thy cheek and cold,
  Colder thy kiss;
Truly that hour foretold
  Sorrow to this.

The dew of the morning
  Sunk chill on my brow—
It felt like the warning
  Of what I feel now.
Thy vows are all broken,
  And light is thy fame;
I hear thy name spoken,
  And share in its shame.

They name thee before me,
  A knell to mine ear;
A shudder comes o'er me—
  Why wert thou so dear?
They know not I knew thee,
  Who knew thee too well:—
Long, long shall I rue thee,
  Too deeply to tell.

In secret we met—
  In silence I grieve
That thy heart could forget,
  Thy spirit deceive.
If I should meet thee
  After long years,
How should I greet thee?—
  With silence and tears.

## "There Was a Time, I Need Not Name"

There was a time, I need not name,
    Since it will ne'er forgotten be,
When all our feelings were the same
    As still my soul hath been to thee.

And from that hour when first thy tongue
    Confess'd a love which equall'd mine,
Though many a grief my heart hath wrung,
    Unknown and thus unfelt by thine,

None, none hath sunk so deep as this—
    To think how all that love hath flown;
Transient as every faithless kiss,
    But transient in thy breast alone.

And yet my heart some solace knew,
    When late I heard thy lips declare,
In accents once imagined true,
    Remembrance of the days that were.

Yes; my adored, yet most unkind!
    Though thou wilt never love again,
To me 't is doubly sweet to find
    Remembrance of that love remain.

Yes! 't is a glorious thought to me,
    Nor longer shall my soul repine,
Whate'er thou art or e'er shalt be,
    Thou hast been dearly, solely mine.

### "And Wilt Thou Weep When
### I Am Low?"

And wilt thou weep when I am low?
  Sweet lady! speak those words again:
Yet if they grieve thee, say not so—
  I would not give that bosom pain.

My heart is sad, my hopes are gone,
  My blood runs coldly through my breast;
And when I perish, thou alone
  Wilt sigh above my place of rest.

And yet, methinks, a gleam of peace
  Doth through my cloud of anguish shine;
  And for awhile my sorrows cease,
  To know thy heart hath felt for mine.

Oh lady! blessed be that tear—
  It falls for one who cannot weep;
Such precious drops are doubly dear
  To those whose eyes no tear may steep.

Sweet lady! once my heart was warm
  With every feeling soft as thine;
But beauty's self hath ceased to charm
  A wretch created to repine.

Yet wilt thou weep when I am low?
　　Sweet lady! speak those words again;
Yet if they grieve thee, say not so—
　　I would not give that bosom pain.

## "Remind Me Not, Remind Me Not"

Remind me not, remind me not,
　　Of those beloved, those vanish'd hours,
　　　　When all my soul was given to thee;
Hours that may never be forgot,
　　Till time unnerves our vital powers,
　　　　And thou and I shall cease to be.

Can I forget—canst thou forget,
　　When playing with thy golden hair,
　　　　How quick thy fluttering heart did move?
Oh! by my soul, I see thee yet,
　　With eyes so languid, breast so fair,
　　　　And lips, though silent, breathing love.

When thus reclining on my breast,
　　Those eyes threw back a glance so sweet,
　　　　As half reproach'd yet raised desire,
And still we near and nearer prest,
　　And still our glowing lips would meet,
　　　　As if in kisses to expire.

And then those pensive eyes would close,
    And bid their lids each other seek,
        Veiling the azure orbs below;
While their long lashes' darken'd gloss
    Seem'd stealing o'er thy brilliant cheek,
        Like raven's plumage smooth'd on snow.

I dreamt last night our love return'd,
    And, sooth to say, that very dream
        Was sweeter in its phantasy,
Than if for other hearts I burn'd,
    For eyes that ne'er like thine could beam
        In rapture's wild reality.

Then tell me not, remind me not,
    Of hours which, though for ever gone,
        Can still a pleasing dream restore,
Till thou and I shall be forgot,
    And senseless as the mouldering stone
        Which tells that we shall be no more.


## Stanzas to a Lady on Leaving England

'T is done—and shivering in the gale
The bark unfurls her snowy sail;
And whistling o'er the bending mast
Loud sings on high the fresh'ning blast;
And I must from this land be gone,
Because I cannot love but one.

But could I be what I have been,
And could I see what I have seen—
Could I repose upon the breast
Which once my warmest wishes blest—
I should not seek another zone,
Because I cannot love but one.

'T is long since I beheld that eye
Which gave me bliss or misery;
And I have striven, but in vain,
Never to think of it again:
For though I fly from Albion,
I still can only love but one.

As some lone bird, without a mate,
My weary heart is desolate;
I look around, and cannot trace
One friendly smile or welcome face,
And ev'n in crowds am still alone,
Because I cannot love but one.

And I will cross the whitening foam,
And I will seek a foreign home;
Till I forget a false fair face,
I ne'er shall find a resting-place;
My own dark thoughts I cannot shun,
But ever love, and love but one.

The poorest, veriest wretch on earth
Still finds some hospitable hearth,
Where friendship's or love's softer glow
May smile in joy or soothe in woe;
But friend or leman I have none,
Because I cannot love but one.

I go—but wheresoe'er I flee
There's not an eye will weep for me;
There's not a kind congenial heart,
Where I can claim the meanest part;
Nor thou, who hast my hopes undone,
Wilt sigh, although I love but one.

To think of every early scene,
Of what we are, and what we've been,
Would whelm some softer hearts with woe—
But mine, alas! has stood the blow;
Yet still beats on as it begun,
And never truly loves but one.

And who that dear loved one may be,
Is not for vulgar eyes to see;
And why that early love was crost,
Thou know'st the best, I feel the most;
But few that dwell beneath the sun
Have loved so long, and loved but one.

I've tried another's fetters too
With charms perchance as fair to view;
And I would fain have loved as well,
But some unconquerable spell
Forbade my bleeding breast to own
A kindred care for aught but one.

'T would soothe to take one lingering view,
And bless thee in my last adieu;
Yet wish I not those eyes to weep
For him that wanders o'er the deep;
His home, his hope, his youth are gone,
Yet still he loves, and loves but one.

## The Girl of Cadiz

Oh never talk again to me
   Of northern climes and British ladies;
It has not been your lot to see,
   Like me, the lovely girl of Cadiz.
Although her eye be not of blue,
   Nor fair her locks, like English lasses,
How far its own expressive hue
   The languid azure eye surpasses!

Prometheus-like, from heaven she stole
   The fire, that through those silken lashes
In darkest glances seem to roll,
   From eyes that cannot hide their flashes:
And as along her bosom steal
   In lengthen'd flow her raven tresses,
You'd swear each clustering lock could feel,
   And curl'd to give her neck caresses.

Our English maids are long to woo,
   And frigid even in possession;
And if their charms be fair to view,
   Their lips are slow at Love's confession:
But, born beneath a brighter sun,
   For love ordain'd the Spanish maid is,
And who,—when fondly, fairly won,—
   Enchants you like the Girl of Cadiz?

The Spanish maid is no coquette,
   Nor joys to see a lover tremble,
And if she love, or if she hate,
   Alike she knows not to dissemble.

Her heart can ne'er be bought or sold—
  Howe'er it beats, it beats sincerely;
And, though it will not bend to gold,
  'T will love you long and love you dearly.


The Spanish girl that meets your love
  Ne'er taunts you with a mock denial,
For every thought is bent to prove
  Her passion in the hour of trial.
When thronging foemen menace Spain,
  She dares the deed and shares the danger;
And should her lover press the plain,
  She hurls the spear, her love's avenger.


And when, beneath the evening star,
  She mingles in the gay Bolero,
Or sings to her attuned guitar
  Of Christian knight or Moorish hero,
Or counts her beads with fairy hand
  Beneath the twinkling rays of Hesper,
Or joins Devotion's choral band,
  To chaunt the sweet and hallow'd vesper;—


In each her charms the heart must move
  Of all who venture to behold her;
Then let not maids less fair reprove
  Because her bosom is not colder:
Through many a clime 't is mine to roam
  Where many a soft and melting maid is,
But none abroad, and few at home,
  May match the dark-eyed Girl of Cadiz.

## *"Maid of Athens, Ere We Part"*

Ζώη μοῦ, σάς ἀγαπῶ.

Maid of Athens, ere we part,
Give, oh, give me back my heart!
Or, since that has left my breast,
Keep it now, and take the rest!
Hear my vow before I go,
Ζώη μοῦ, σάς ἀγαπῶ.

By those tresses unconfined,
Woo'd by each Ægean wind;
By those lids whose jetty fringe
Kiss thy soft cheeks' blooming tinge;
By those wild eyes like the roe,
Ζώη μοῦ, σάς ἀγαπῶ.

By that lip I long to taste;
By that zone-encircled waist;
By all the token-flowers that tell
What words can never speak so well;
By love's alternate joy and woe,
Ζώη μοῦ, σάς ἀγαπῶ.

Maid of Athens! I am gone:
Think of me, sweet! when alone.
Though I fly to Istambol,
Athens holds my heart and soul:
Can I cease to love thee? No!
Ζώη μοῦ, σάς ἀγαπῶ.

Theresa Macri as "The Maid of Athens"

## On Parting

The kiss, dear maid! thy lip has left
   Shall never part from mine,
Till happier hours restore the gift
   Untainted back to thine.

Thy parting glance, which fondly beams,
   An equal love may see;
The tear that from thine eyelid streams
   Can weep no change in me.

I ask no pledge to make me blest
   In gazing when alone;
Nor one memorial for a breast,
   Whose thoughts are all thine own.

Nor need I write—to tell the tale
   My pen were doubly weak:
Oh! what can idle words avail,
   Unless the heart could speak?

By day or night, in weal or woe,
   That heart, no longer free,
Must bear the love it cannot show,
   And silent ache for thee.

Lady Caroline Lamb

### "And Thou Art Dead, as Young and Fair"

Heu, quanto minus est cum reliquis versari
quam tui meminisse!

And thou art dead, as young and fair
As aught of mortal birth;
And form so soft, and charms so rare,
Too soon return'd to Earth!
Though Earth received them in her bed,
And o'er the spot the crowd may tread
In carelessness or mirth,
There is an eye which could not brook
A moment on that grave to look.

I will not ask where thou liest low,
Nor gaze upon the spot;
There flowers or weeds at will may grow,
So I behold them not:
It is enough for me to prove
That what I loved, and long must love,
Like common earth can rot;
To me there needs no stone to tell,
'T is Nothing that I loved so well.

Yet did I love thee to the last
    As fervently as thou,
Who didst not change through all the past
    And canst not alter now.
The love where Death has set his seal,
Nor age can chill, nor rival steal,
    Nor falsehood disavow:
And, what were worse, thou canst not see
Or wrong, or change, or fault in me.

The better days of life were ours;
    The worst can be but mine:
The sun that cheers, the storm that lowers,
    Shall never more be thine.
The silence of that dreamless sleep
I envy now too much to weep;
    Nor need I to repine
That all those charms have pass'd away,
I might have watch'd through long decay.

The flower in ripen'd bloom unmatch'd
    Must fall the earliest prey;
Though by no hand untimely snatch'd,
    The leaves must drop away:
And yet it were a greater grief
To watch it withering, leaf by leaf,
    Than see it pluck'd to-day;
Since earthly eye but ill can bear
To trace the change to foul from fair.

I know not if I could have borne
　　To see thy beauties fade;
The night that follow'd such a morn
　　Had worn a deeper shade:
Thy day without a cloud hath pass'd,
And thou wert lovely to the last,
　　Extinguish'd, not decay'd;
As stars that shoot along the sky
Shine brightest as they fall from high.

As once I wept, if I could weep,
　　My tears might well be shed,
To think I was not near to keep
　　One vigil o'er thy bed;
To gaze, how fondly! on thy face,
To fold thee in a faint embrace,
　　Uphold thy drooping head;
And show that love, however vain,
Nor thou nor I can feel again.

Yet how much less it were to gain,
　　Though thou hast left me free,
The loveliest things that still remain,
　　Than thus remember thee!
The all of thine that cannot die
Through dark and dread Eternity
　　Returns again to me,
And more thy buried love endears
Than aught, except its living years.

### On Being Asked What Was the "Origin of Love"

The "Origin of Love!"—Ah! why
    That cruel question ask of me,
When thou mayst read in many an eye
    He starts to life on seeing thee?

And shouldst thou seek his *end* to know:
    My heart forebodes, my fears foresee,
He'll linger long in silent woe;
    But live—until I cease to be.

### "Remember Him Whom Passion's Power"

Remember him whom passion's power
    Severely, deeply, vainly proved:
Remember thou that dangerous hour
    When neither fell, though both were loved.

That yielding breast, that melting eye,
    Too much invited to be bless'd:
That gentle prayer, that pleading sigh,
    The wilder wish reproved, repress'd.

Oh! let me feel that all I lost
    But saved thee all that conscience fears;
And blush for every pang it cost
    To spare the vain remorse of years.

Yet think of this when many a tongue,
   Whose busy accents whisper blame,
Would do the heart that loved thee wrong,
   And brand a nearly blighted name.

Think that, whate'er to others, thou
   Hast seen each selfish thought subdued:
I bless thy purer soul even now,
   Even now, in midnight solitude.

Oh God! that we had met in time,
   Our hearts as fond, thy hand more free;
When thou hadst loved without a crime,
   And I been less unworthy thee!

Far may thy days, as heretofore,
   From this our gaudy world be past!
And that too bitter moment o'er,
   Oh, may such trial be thy last!

This heart, alas! perverted long,
   Itself destroy'd might there destroy;
To meet thee in the glittering throng,
   Would wake Presumption's hope of joy.

Then to the things whose bliss or woe,
   Like mine, is wild and worthless all,
That world resign—such scenes forego,
   Where those who feel must surely fall.

Thy youth, thy charms, thy tenderness,
   Thy soul from long seclusion pure;
From what even here hath pass'd, may guess
   What there thy bosom must endure.

Oh! pardon that imploring tear,
   Since not by Virtue shed in vain,
My frenzy drew from eyes so dear;
   For me they shall not weep again.

Though long and mournful must it be,
   The thought that we no more may meet;
Yet I deserve the stern decree,
   And almost deem the sentence sweet.

Still, had I loved thee less, my heart
   Had then less sacrificed to thine;
It felt not half so much to part,
   As if its guilt had made thee mine.

### Love and Gold

I cannot talk of Love to thee,
   Though thou art young and free and fair!
There is a spell thou dost not see,
   That bids a genuine love despair.

And yet that spell invites each youth,
   For thee to sigh, or seem to sigh;
Makes falsehood wear the garb of truth,
   And Truth itself appear a lie.

If ever Doubt a place possest
   In woman's heart, 't were wise in thine:
Admit not Love into thy breast,
   Doubt others' love, nor trust in mine.

Perchance 't is feign'd, perchance sincere,
    But false or true thou canst not tell;
So much hast thou from all to fear,
    In that unconquerable spell.

Of all the herd that throng around,
    Thy simpering or thy sighing train,
Come tell me who to thee is bound
    By Love's or Plutus' heavier chain.

In some 't is Nature, some 't is Art
    That bids them worship at thy shrine;
But thou deserv'st a better heart,
    Than they or I can give for thine.

For thee, and such as thee, behold,
    Is Fortune painted truly—blind!
Who doom'd thee to be bought or sold,
    Has proved too bounteous to be kind.

Each day some tempter's crafty suit
    Would woo thee to a loveless bed:
I see thee to the altar's foot
    A decorated victim led.

Adieu, dear maid! I must not speak
    Whate'er my secret thoughts may be;
Though thou art all that man can reck
    I dare not talk of Love to *thee*.

Margarita Cogni

## Stanzas for Music

There be none of Beauty's daughters
  With a magic like thee;
And like music on the waters
  Is thy sweet voice to me:
When, as if its sound were causing
The charmèd ocean's pausing,
The waves lie still and gleaming,
And the lull'd winds seem dreaming.

And the midnight moon is weaving
  Her bright chain o'er the deep;
Whose breast is gently heaving,
  As an infant's asleep:
So the spirit bows before thee,
To listen and adore thee;
With a full but soft emotion,
Like the swell of Summer's ocean.

## "She Walks in Beauty"

She walks in beauty, like the night
   Of cloudless climes and starry skies;
And all that's best of dark and bright
   Meet in her aspect and her eyes:
Thus mellow'd to that tender light
   Which heaven to gaudy day denies.

One shade the more, one ray the less,
   Had half impair'd the nameless grace
Which waves in every raven tress,
   Or softly lightens o'er her face;
Where thoughts serenely sweet express
   How pure, how dear their dwelling-place.

And on that cheek, and o'er that brow,
   So soft, so calm, yet eloquent,
The smiles that win, the tints that glow,
   But tell of days in goodness spent,
A mind at peace with all below,
   A heart whose love is innocent!

## "Oh! Snatch'd Away in Beauty's Bloom"

Oh! snatch'd away in beauty's bloom,
On thee shall press no ponderous tomb;
  But on thy turf shall roses rear
  Their leaves, the earliest of the year;
And the wild cypress wave in tender gloom:

And oft by yon blue gushing stream
  Shall Sorrow lean her drooping head,
And feed deep thought with many a dream,
  And lingering pause and lightly tread;
  Fond wretch! as if her step disturb'd the dead!

Away! we know that tears are vain,
  That death nor heeds nor hears distress;
Will this unteach us to complain?
  Or make one mourner weep the less?
And thou—who tell'st me to forget,
Thy looks are wan, thine eyes are wet.

Augusta Ada Byron

### Stanzas for Music

They say that Hope is happiness;
  But genuine Love must prize the past,
And Memory wakes the thoughts that bless;
  They rose the first—they set the last.

And all that Memory loves the most
  Was once our only Hope to be,
And all that Hope adored and lost
  Hath melted into Memory.

Alas! it is delusion all;
  The future cheats us from afar,
Nor can we be what we recall,
  Nor dare we think on what we are.

Lady Noel Byron

## Fare Thee Well

Alas! they had been friends in Youth;
But whispering tongues can poison truth:
And constancy lives in realms above;
And Life is thorny; and youth is vain;
And to be wroth with one we love,
Doth work like madness in the brain;

.    .    .    .    .    .    .    .    .    .

But never either found another
To free the hollow heart from paining—
They stood aloof, the scars remaining,
Like cliffs, which had been rent asunder;
A dreary sea now flows between,
But neither heat, nor frost, nor thunder,
Shall wholly do away, I ween,
The marks of that which once hath been.
                         —Coleridge, *Christabel*

Fare thee well! and if for ever,
    Still for ever, fare *thee well*:
Even though unforgiving, never
    'Gainst thee shall my heart rebel.

Would that breast were bared before thee
    Where thy head so oft hath lain,
Where that placid sleep came o'er thee
    Which thou ne'er canst know again:

Would that breast, by thee glanced over,
    Every inmost thought could show!
Then thou wouldst at last discover
    'T was not well to spurn it so.

Though the world for this commend thee—
    Though it smile upon the blow,
Even its praises must offend thee,
    Founded on another's woe:

Though my many faults defaced me,
    Could no other arm be found,
Than the one which once embraced me,
    To inflict a cureless wound?

Yet, oh yet, thyself deceive not;
    Love may sink by slow decay,
But by sudden wrench, believe not
    Hearts can thus be torn away:

Still thine own its life retaineth—
    Still must mine, though bleeding, beat;
And the undying thought which paineth
    Is—that we no more may meet.

These are words of deeper sorrow
    Than the wail above the dead;
Both shall live, but every morrow
    Wake us from a widow'd bed.

And when thou wouldst solace gather,
    When our child's first accents flow,
Wilt thou teach her to say "Father!"
    Though his care she must forego?

When her little hands shall press thee,
    When her lip to thine is press'd,
Think of him whose prayer shall bless thee,
    Think of him thy love had bless'd!

Should her lineaments resemble
    Those thou nevermore may'st see,
Then thy heart will softly tremble
    With a pulse yet true to me.

All my faults perchance thou knowest,
    All my madness none can know;
All my hopes, where'er thou goest,
    Wither, yet with *thee* they go.

Every feeling hath been shaken;
    Pride, which not a world could bow,
Bows to thee—by thee forsaken,
    Even my soul forsakes me now:

But 't is done—all words are idle—
    Words from me are vainer still;
But the thoughts we cannot bridle
    Force their way without the will.

Fare thee well!—thus disunited,
    Torn from every nearer tie,
Sear'd in heart, and lone, and blighted,
    More than this I scarce can die.

## Stanzas to Augusta

Though the day of my destiny's over,
  And the star of my fate hath declined,
Thy soft heart refused to discover
  The faults which so many could find;
Though thy soul with my grief was acquainted,
  It shrunk not to share it with me,
And the love which my spirit hath painted
  It never hath found but in *thee*.

Then when nature around me is smiling,
  The last smile which answers to mine,
I do not believe it beguiling,
  Because it reminds me of thine;
And when winds are at war with the ocean,
  As the breasts I believed in with me,
If their billows excite an emotion,
  It is that they bear me from *thee*.

Though the rock of my last hope is shiver'd,
  And its fragments are sunk in the wave,
Though I feel that my soul is deliver'd
  To pain—it shall not be its slave.
There is many a pang to pursue me:
  They may crush, but they shall not contemn—
They may torture, but shall not subdue me—
  'T is of *thee* that I think—not of them.

Though human, thou didst not deceive me,
  Though woman, thou didst not forsake,
Though loved, thou forborest to grieve me,
  Though slander'd, thou never couldst shake,—
Though trusted, thou didst not disclaim me,
  Though parted, it was not to fly,
Though watchful, 't was not to defame me,
  Nor, mute, that the world might belie.

Yet I blame not the world, nor despise it,
  Nor the war of the many with one—
If my soul was not fitted to prize it,
  'T was folly not sooner to shun:
And if dearly that error hath cost me,
  And more than I once could foresee,
I have found that, whatever it lost me,
  It could not deprive me of *thee*.

From the wreck of the past, which hath perish'd,
  Thus much I at least may recall,
It hath taught me that what I most cherish'd
  Deserved to be dearest of all:
In the desert a fountain is springing,
  In the wide waste there still is a tree,
And a bird in the solitude singing,
  Which speaks to my spirit of *thee*.

## *So We'll Go No More A-Roving*

### 1

So we'll go no more a-roving
  So late into the night,
Though the heart be still as loving,
  And the moon be still as bright.

### 2

For the sword outwears its sheath,
  And the soul wears out the breast,
And the heart must pause to breathe,
  And Love itself have rest.

### 3

Though the night was made for loving,
  And the day returns too soon,
Yet we'll go no more a-roving
  By the light of the moon.

## Stanzas to the Po

River, that rollest by the ancient walls,
　　Where dwells the lady of my love, when she
Walks by thy brink, and there perchance recalls
　　A faint and fleeting memory of me;

What if thy deep and ample stream should be
　　A mirror of my heart, where she may read
The thousand thoughts I now betray to thee,
　　Wild as thy wave, and headlong as thy speed!

What do I say—a mirror of my heart?
　　Are not thy waters sweeping, dark, and strong?
Such as my feelings were and are, thou art;
　　And such as thou art were my passions long.

Time may have somewhat tamed them,—not for ever;
　　Thou overflow'st thy banks, and not for aye
Thy bosom overboils, congenial river!
　　Thy floods subside, and mine have sunk away—

But left long wrecks behind: and now again,
　　Borne in our old unchanged career, we move;
Thou tendest wildly onwards to the main.
　　And I—to loving *one* I should not love.

The current I behold will sweep beneath
　　Her native walls and murmur at her feet;
Her eyes will look on thee, when she shall breathe
　　The twilight air, unharm'd by summer's heat.

She will look on thee,—I have look'd on thee,
　　Full of that thought; and, from that moment, ne'er
Thy waters could I dream of, name, or see,
　　Without the inseparable sigh for her!

Her bright eyes will be imaged in thy stream,—
    Yes! they will meet the wave I gaze on now:
Mine cannot witness, even in a dream,
    That happy wave repass me in its flow!


The wave that bears my tears returns no more:
    Will she return by whom that wave shall sweep?—
Both tread thy banks, both wander on thy shore,
    I by thy source, she by the dark-blue deep.


But that which keepeth us apart is not
    Distance, nor depth of wave, nor space of earth,
But the distraction of a various lot,
    As various as the climates of our birth.


A stranger loves the lady of the land,
    Born far beyond the mountains, but his blood
Is all meridian, as if never fann'd
    By the black wind that chills the polar flood.


My blood is all meridian; were it not,
    I had not left my clime, nor should I be,
In spite of tortures, ne'er to be forgot,
    A slave again of love,—at least of thee.


'T is vain to struggle—let me perish young—
    Live as I lived, and love as I have loved;
To dust if I return, from dust I sprung,
    And then, at least, my heart can ne'er be moved.

### Sonnet on the Nuptials of the Marquis Antonio Cavalli with the Countess Clelia Rasponi of Ravenna

A noble Lady of the Italian shore,
  Lovely and young, herself a happy bride,
  Commands a verse, and will not be denied,
From me a wandering Englishman; I tore
One sonnet, but invoke the muse once more
  To hail these gentle hearts which Love has tied,
  In Youth, Birth, Beauty, genially allied,
And blest with Virtue's soul and Fortune's store.
A sweeter language and a luckier bard
  Were worthier of your hopes, Auspicious Pair!
And of the sanctity of Hymen's shrine,
  But,—since I cannot but obey the Fair,
To render your new state your true reward,
May your Fate be like *Hers*, and unlike *mine*.

### Stanzas

Could Love for ever
Run like a river,
And Time's endeavour
  Be tried in vain—
No other pleasure
With this could measure,
And like a treasure
  We'd hug the chain.
But since our sighing

Ends not in dying,
And, form'd for flying,
　Love plumes his wing;
Then for this reason
Let's love a season;
But let that season be only Spring.

When lovers parted
Feel broken-hearted,
And, all hopes thwarted,
　Expect to die;
A few years older,
Ah! how much colder
They might behold her
　For whom they sigh!
When link'd together,
In every weather,
They pluck Love's feather
　From out his wing—
He'll stay for ever,
But sadly shiver
Without his plumage, when past the Spring.

Like Chiefs of Faction,
His life is action—
A formal paction
　That curbs his reign,
Obscures his glory,
Despot no more, he
Such territory
　Quits with disdain.
Still, still advancing,
With banners glancing,
His power enhancing,
　He must move on—

Repose but cloys him,
Retreat destroys him,
Love brooks not a degraded throne.


Wait not, fond lover!
Till years are over,
And then recover,
    As from a dream.
While each bewailing
The other's failing,
With wrath and railing,
    All hideous seem—
While first decreasing,
Yet not quite ceasing,
Wait not till teasing
    All passion blight:
If once diminish'd
Love's reign is finish'd—
Then part in friendship,   and bid goodnight.


So shall Affection
To recollection
The dear connection
    Bring back with joy:
You had not waited
Till, tired or hated,
Your passions sated
    Began to cloy.
Your last embraces
Leave no cold traces—
The same fond faces
    As through the past;
And eyes, the mirrors
Of your sweet errors,
Reflect but rapture—not least though last.

True, separations
Ask more than patience;
What desperations
  From such have risen!
But yet remaining,
What is 't but chaining
Hearts which, once waning,
  Beat 'gainst their prison?
Time can but cloy love,
And use destroy love:
The wingèd boy, Love,
  Is but for boys—
You'll find it torture
Though sharper, shorter,
To wean, and not wear out your joys.

Teresa Guiccioli

## Stanzas to a Hindoo Air

Oh!—my lonely—lonely—lonely—Pillow!
Where is my lover, where is my lover?
Is it his bark which my dreary dreams discover?
   Far—far away! and alone along the billow?

Oh! my lonely—lonely—lonely—Pillow!
Why must my head ache where his gentle brow lay?
How the long night flags lovelessly and slowly,
   And my head droops over thee like the willow!

Oh! thou, my sad and solitary Pillow!
Send me kind dreams to keep my heart from breaking,
In return for the tears I shed upon thee waking;
   Let me not die till he comes back o'er the billow.

Then if thou wilt—no more my *lonely* Pillow,
In one embrace let these arms again enfold him,
And then expire of the joy—but to behold him!
   Oh! my lone bosom!—oh! my lonely Pillow!

## To ———

But once I dared to lift my eyes,
    To lift my eyes to thee;
And, since that day, beneath the skies,
    No other sight they see.

In vain sleep shuts them in the night,
    The night grows day to me,
Presenting idly to my sight
    What still a dream must be.

A fatal dream—for many a bar
    Divides thy fate from mine;
And still my passions wake and war,
    But peace be still with thine.


## On This Day I Complete My Thirty-Sixth Year

'T is time this heart should be unmoved,
    Since others it hath ceased to move:
Yet, though I cannot be beloved,
        Still let me love!

My days are in the yellow leaf;
    The flowers and fruits of love are gone;
The worm, the canker, and the grief
        Are mine alone!

The fire that on my bosom preys
  Is lone as some volcanic isle;
No torch is kindled at its blaze—
    A funeral pile.

The hope, the fear, the jealous care,
  The exalted portion of the pain
And power of love, I cannot share,
    But wear the chain.

But 't is not *thus*—and 't is not *here*—
  Such thoughts should shake my soul, nor *now*,
Where glory decks the hero's bier,
    Or binds his brow.

The sword, the banner, and the field,
  Glory and Greece, around me see!
The Spartan, borne upon his shield,
    Was not more free.

Awake! (not Greece—she *is* awake!)
  Awake, my spirit! Think through *whom*
Thy life-blood tracks its parent lake,
    And then strike home!

Tread those reviving passions down,
  Unworthy manhood!—unto thee
Indifferent should the smile or frown
    Of beauty be.

If thou regret'st thy youth, *why live?*
  The land of honourable death
Is here:—up to the field, and give
    Away thy breath!

Seek out—less often sought than found—
     A soldier's grave, for thee the best;
Then look around, and choose thy ground,
          And take thy rest.

# Notes

The date of composition and date of first publication follow the poem title and the page reference.

**To Caroline** (p. 1) 1805. *First Poems* (1806). Caroline is a generic name.

**To Caroline** (p. 2) 1805. *First Poems* (1806). The identity of Mary is unknown. She is not Mary Chaworth. See p. 11 for Mary Chaworth's likeness.

**Imitated from Catallus** (p. 3) November 16, 1806. *First Poems* (1806). An imitation of Catullus's *Carmina*, XLVIII, "Melitos oculos tuos, Juventi," which translates to "Your honeyed eyes, Juventius. . . ."

**From Anacreon** (p. 4) 1805 or 1806. *Hours of Idleness: A Series of Poems Original and Translated* (1807). The Greek epigraph is from *Anacreontea*, Poem 23, line 1, which translates to "I want to speak of the sons of Atreus. . . ." The epigraph is not by Anacreon, but rather comes from the *Anacreontea*, a late (anywhere from 1st to 4th Century A.D.) collection of poems about and in the style of Anacreon.

**To Emma** (p. 5) 1805. *First Poems* (1806). This is a dramatic imagining of Byron's last visit with Mary Chaworth before her marriage in August 1805. See p. 11.

**To M. S. G.** (p. 6) Probably November–December 1806. *Poems on Various Occasions* (1807). Probably addressed to Elizabeth Pigot.

**The First Kiss of Love** (p. 8) December 23, 1806. *Poems on Various Occasions* (1807). The Greek epigraph is from *Anacreontea*,

Poem 23, lines 3–4, which translates to "The lyre with its strings / Echoes only Eros."

**To Woman** (p. 9) Probably 1805 or early 1806. *First Poems* (1806). The poem is derivative of Thomas Moore's "Inconstancy" and the final line derives from a Spanish proverb.

**To M. S. G.** (p. 10) Probably November–December 1806. *Poems on Various Occasions* (1807). Probably addressed to Elizabeth Pigot.

**To Mary on Receiving Her Picture** (p. 12) Written before September 1806. *First Poems* (1806). This poem is addressed to the unknown Mary.

**To Lesbia** (p. 13) 1806. *First Poems* (1806). Lesbia is a generic name. The poem was addressed to Julia Leacroft.

**To a Lady Who Presented to the Author a Lock of Hair Braided with His Own, and Appointed a Night in December to Meet Him in the Garden** (p. 15) Probably December 1805. *First Poems* (1806). This poem is addressed to the unknown Mary.

**Translation from the** *Medea* **of Euripides** (p. 16) April–May 1807. *Hours of Idleness. A Series of Poems Original and Translated* (1807). This poem represents a loose translation of *Medea* (lines 627–60), and the epigraph, taken from line 627, translates to "When love comes in excess. . . ."

**To a Beautiful Quaker** (p. 18) September 1806. *First Poems* (1806). The young lady was seen by Byron at Harrowgate.

**To a Lady Who Presented the Author with the Velvet Band which Bound Her Tresses** (p. 20) 1806. First published in 1832 and apparently addressed to the unknown Mary. The final eight lines comprise a separate poem, "A Woman's Hair," which is addressed to Elizabeth Pigot.

**To a Lady** (p. 21) Probably late 1806 or 1807. *Hours of Idleness. A Series of Poems Original and Translated* (1807). Addressed to Mrs. Chaworth Musters, née Mary Chaworth. See p. 11.

**To Anne** (p. 23) January 16, 1807. First published in 1832. Addressed to Anne Houson.

**On Finding a Fan** (p. 24) 1807. First published in 1832. The fan belonged to Anne Houson.

**Song** (p. 25) July 23, 1808. First published in 1898. Probably addressed to Miss Cameron.

**"When We Two Parted"** (p. 26) August or September 1815. First published in 1815 by Isaac Nathan. Byron misleadingly indicated that he wrote this poem in 1808. Probably addressed to Lady Frances Wedderburn Webster.

**"There Was a Time, I Need Not Name"** (p. 27) June 10, 1808. *Imitations and Translations from the ancient and modern classics* (1809).

**"And Wilt Thou Weep When I am Low?"** (p. 28) August 12, 1808. *Imitations and Translations from the ancient and modern classics* (1809). Addressed to Miss Cameron.

**"Remind Me Not, Remind Me Not"** (p. 29) August 13, 1808, the first five stanzas were written the previous day. *Imitations and Translations from the ancient and modern classics* (1809).

**Stanzas to a Lady on Leaving England** (p. 30) Probably late June 1809. *Imitations and Translations from the ancient and modern classics* (1809). Addressed to Mrs. Chaworth Musters, née Mary Chaworth, and written two days before Byron sailed for Lisbon with John Cam Hobhouse. See p. 11.

**The Girl of Cadiz** (p. 33) August 25, 1809. First published in 1832. Byron composed this poem under sail from Gibraltar to Sardinia.

**"Maid of Athens, Ere We Part"** (p. 35) February 9, 1810 (Athens). *Childe Harold's Pilgrimage: Cantos I–II* (1812). The Maid was twelve-year-old Theresa Macri. See p. 36 for her likeness. Byron translated the Greek as "My Life, I love you!"; the source for the epigraph and refrain is Juvenal's *Satire VI*, line 195.

**On Parting** (p. 37) March 1811. *Childe Harold's Pilgrimage: Cantos I–II* (1812). A farewell lyric addressed to Theresa Macri. See p. 36.

**"And Thou Art Dead, as Young and Fair"** (p. 39) February

1812. *Childe Harold's Pilgrimage: Canto III* (1816). The Latin epigraph translates to "Alas, how much less it is to spend time with others than to remember you!" Probably a reflection on the death of John Edleston.

**On Being Asked What Was the "Origin of Love"** (p. 42) Probably April 1813. First published in 1814. Addressed to Lady Charlotte Harley, daughter of Lady Oxford.

**"Remember Him Whom Passion's Power"** (p. 42) Late October 1813. First published in 1814. Addressed to Lady Frances Wedderburn Webster.

**Love and Gold** (p. 44) 1812–1813. First published in 1900. Possibly addressed to Annabella Milbanke, Byron's future wife. See p. 52 for her likeness.

**Stanzas for Music** (p. 47) March 28, 1816. *Poems 1816*. Probably addressed to Claire Clairmont.

**"She Walks in Beauty"** (p. 48) June 12, 1814. First published in 1815. Written about Mrs. Anne Wilmot, Byron's cousin. Byron saw her at a party and wrote that she "appeared in mourning, with dark spangles on her dress."

**"Oh! Snatch'd Away in Beauty's Bloom"** (p. 49) September–October 1814. First published in *A Selection of Hebrew Melodies, No. I* (1815). Probably a reminiscence of John Edleston.

**Stanzas for Music** (p. 51) Probably late 1814. *A Selection of Hebrew Melodies, Nos. I–IV* (1827–29).

**Fare Thee Well** (p. 53) March 18, 1816. Written about Lady Byron the day after the preliminary separation agreement was signed. Byron had the poem privately printed (50 copies) on April 8, and sent Lady Byron a copy, but the gesture failed to gain a reconciliation and the final separation papers were signed on April 21. Byron authorized the poem's publication in *Poems 1816* and added the Coleridge epigraph.

**Stanzas to Augusta** (p. 56) July 24, 1816. *The Prisoner of Chillon and other poems* (1816). This is another poem about the marriage separation. Addressed to Augusta Leigh, Byron's half sister.

**So We'll Go No More A-Roving** (p. 58) February 28, 1817, after his twenty-ninth birthday (in a letter to Thomas Moore). *Letters and Journals of Lord Byron: with notices of his life* (Vol II, 1830) by Thomas Moore. The refrain of a Scottish song, "The Jolly Beggar" ("And we'll gang nae mair a roving / Sae late into the nicht"), provided the impetus for this poem.

**Stanzas to the Po** (p. 59) June 1 or 2, 1819. First published in *Journal of the Conversations of Lord Byron* (1824). This love lyric is Byron's reflection on his love for the Countess Teresa Guiccioli, after her husband forced her to leave Venice. Their affair began in April in Venice. See p. 63 for a likeness of Countess Guiccioli.

**Sonnet on the Nuptials of the Marquis Antonio Cavalli with the Countess Clelia Rasponi of Ravenna** (p. 61) July 31, 1819 (Ravenna). First published in 1901. Cavalli was the Countess Teresa Guiccioli's uncle and she urged Byron to write the epithalamium. See p. 63.

**Stanzas** (p. 61) December 1, 1819. First published by Lady Blessington in her serialized "Conversations with Lord Byron" in *New Monthly Magazine* 35 (1832). The poem was written when Byron thought that he and the Countess Guiccioli might have to end their affair. See p. 63.

**Stanzas to a Hindoo Air** (p. 66) January 1, 1822. First published in 1832. Written to the Hindustani air of "Alla Malla Punca," which the Countess Guiccioli enjoyed singing. See p. 63.

**To ——** (p. 67) April–May 1823. First published in 1833. This poem was given to Lady Blessington.

**On This Day I Complete My Thirty-Sixth Year** (p. 67) January 22, 1824, (Missolonghi). First published in *The Morning Chronicle* (1824).